Chimpanzee

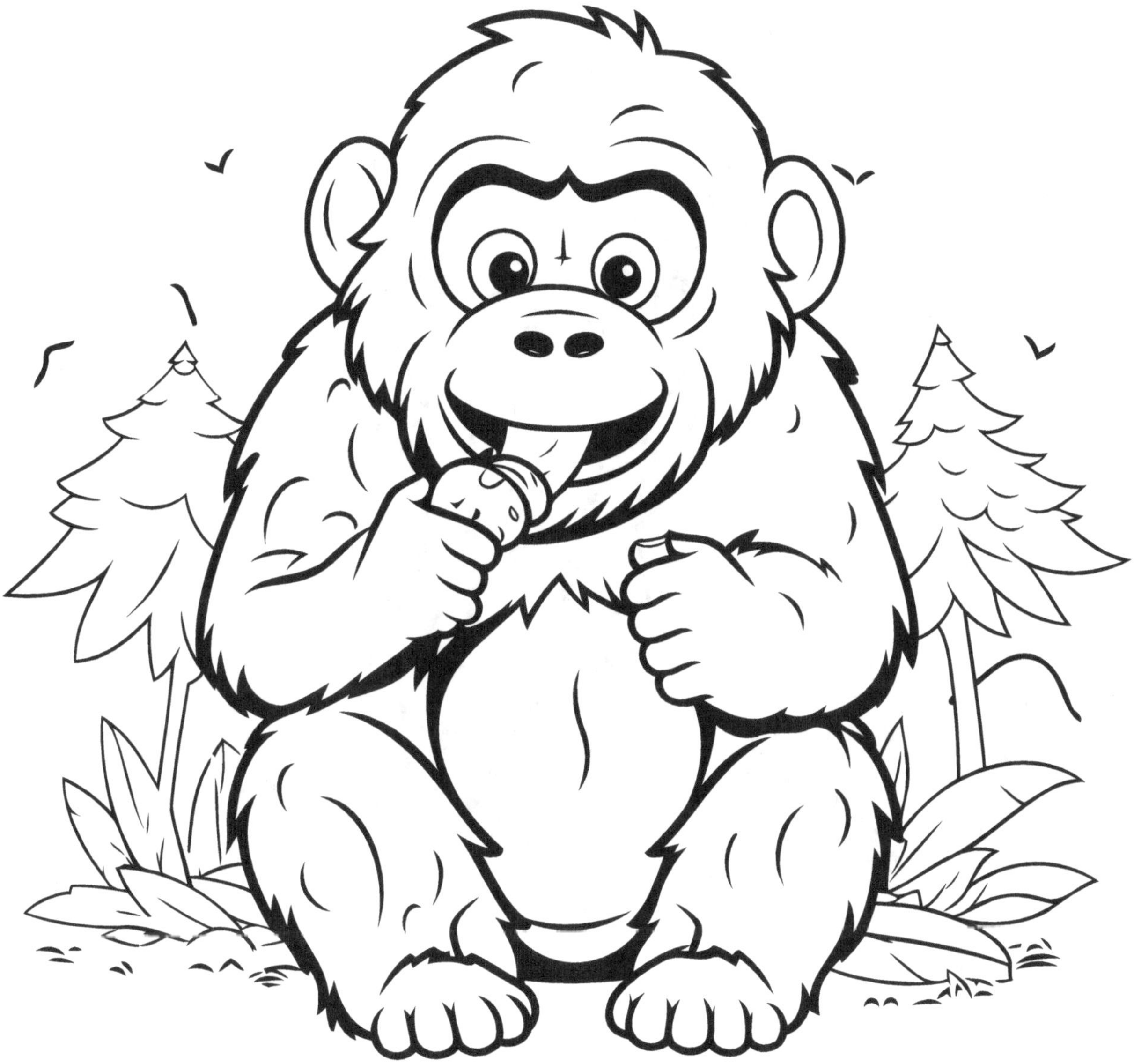

Elephant

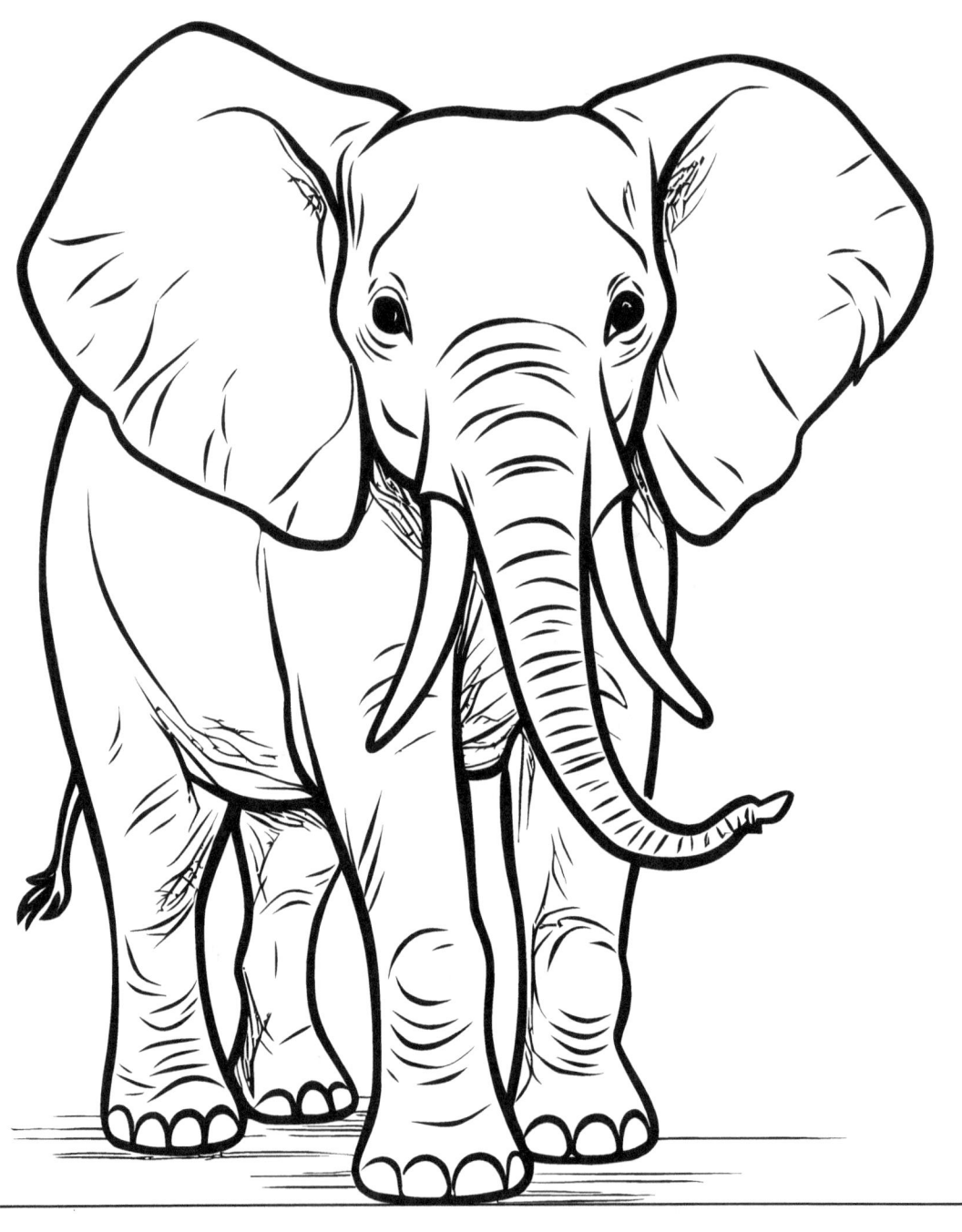

Horse

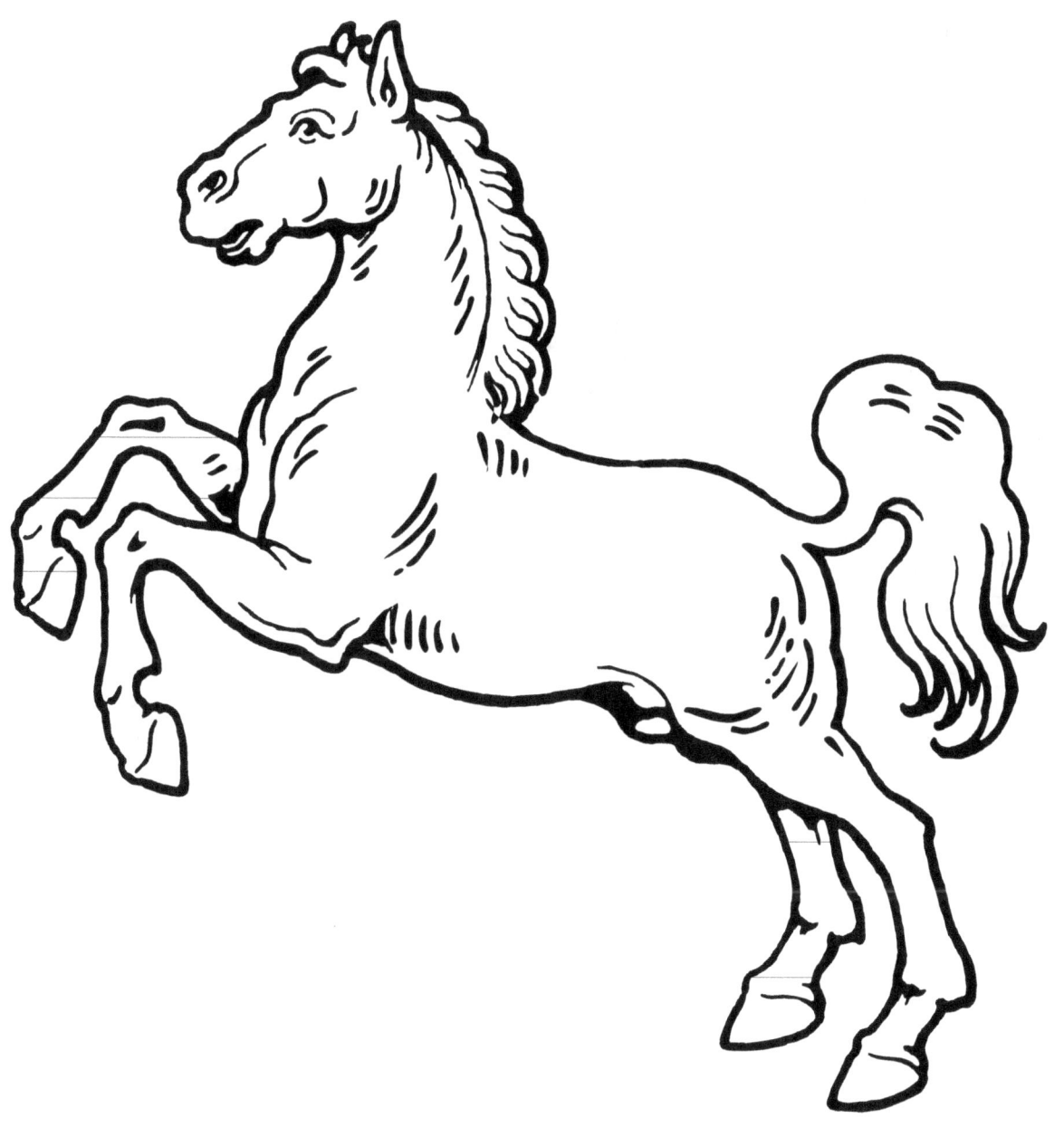

Camel

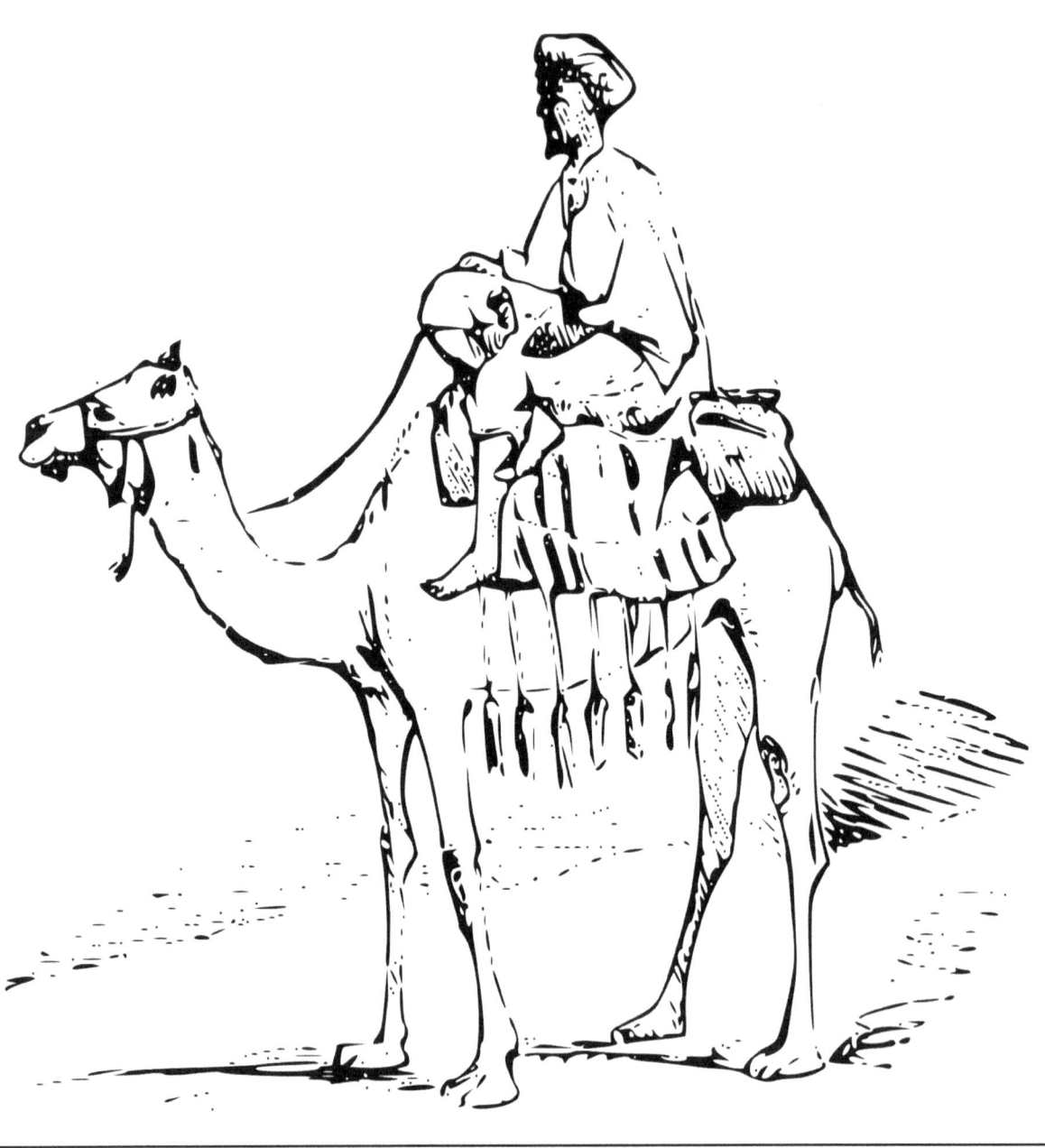

Lion

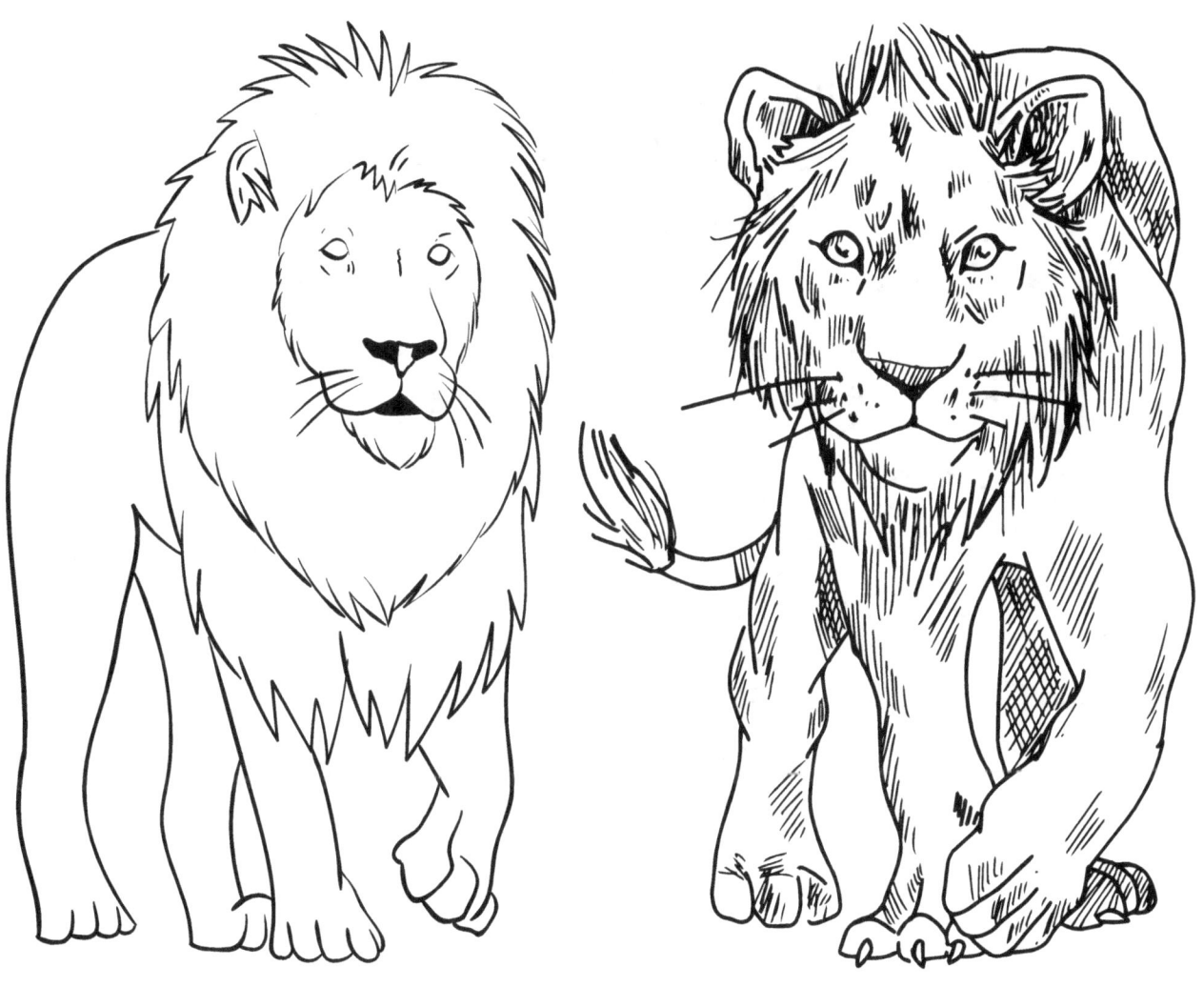

Tiger

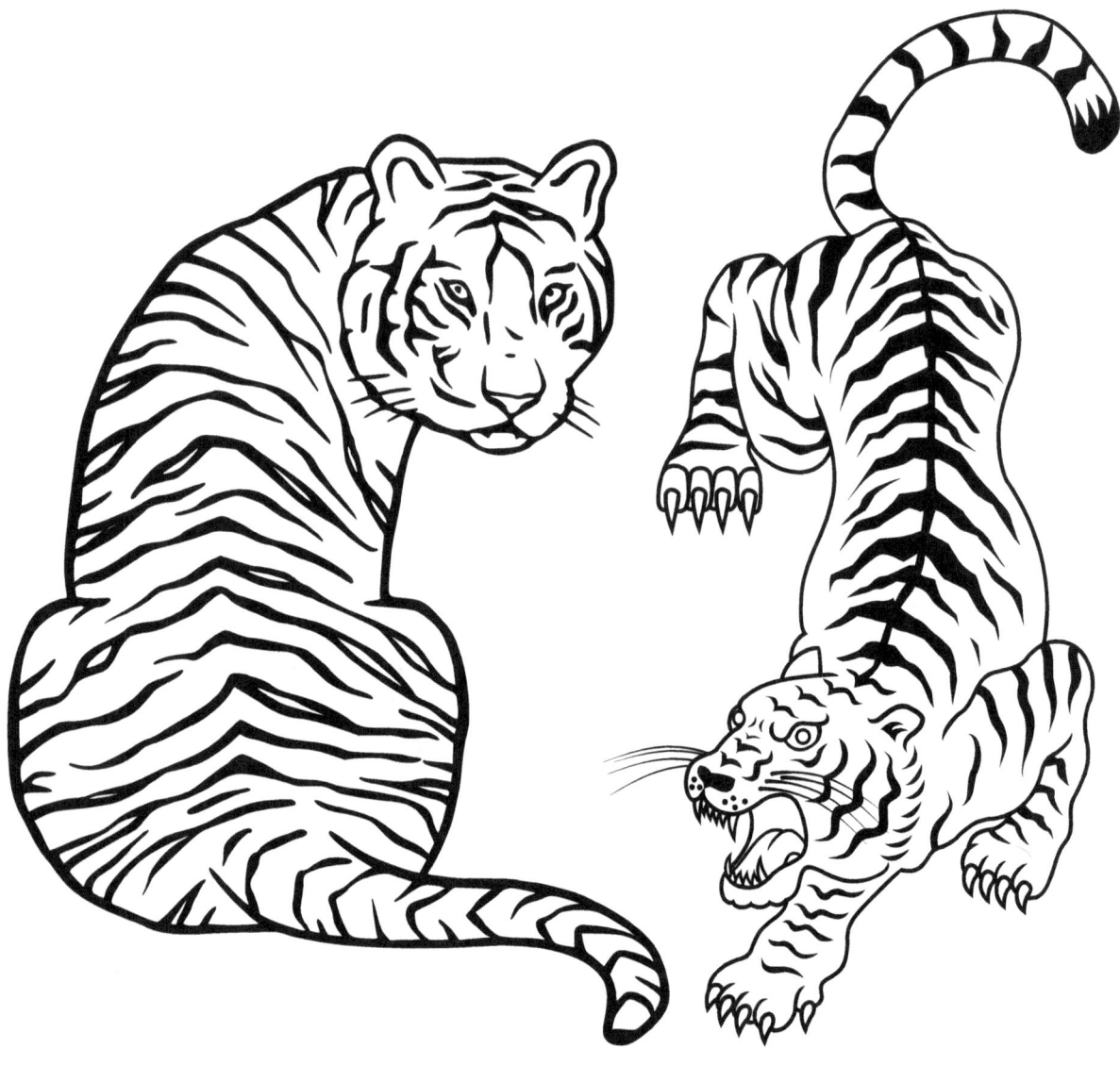

Giraffe

Bear

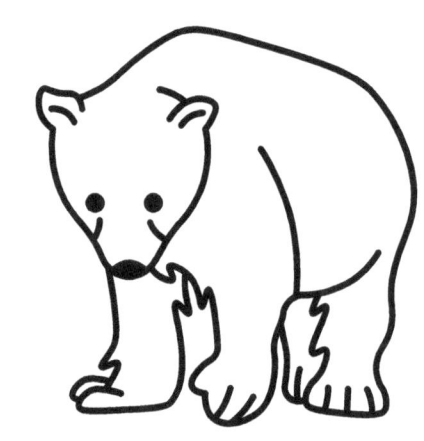

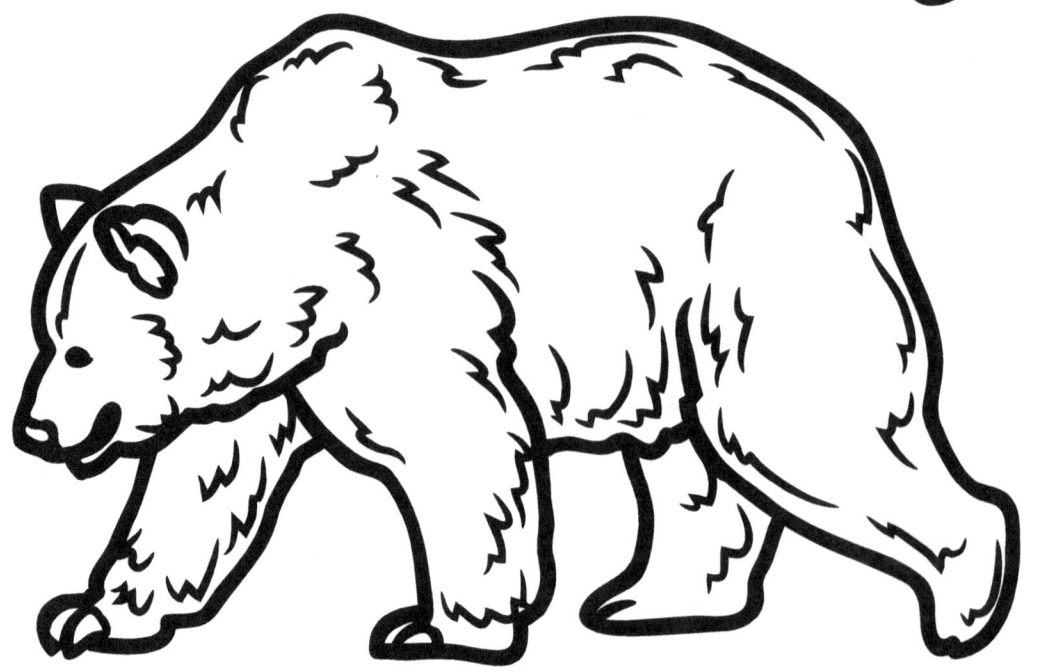

Wolf

Fox

Gazelle

Donkey

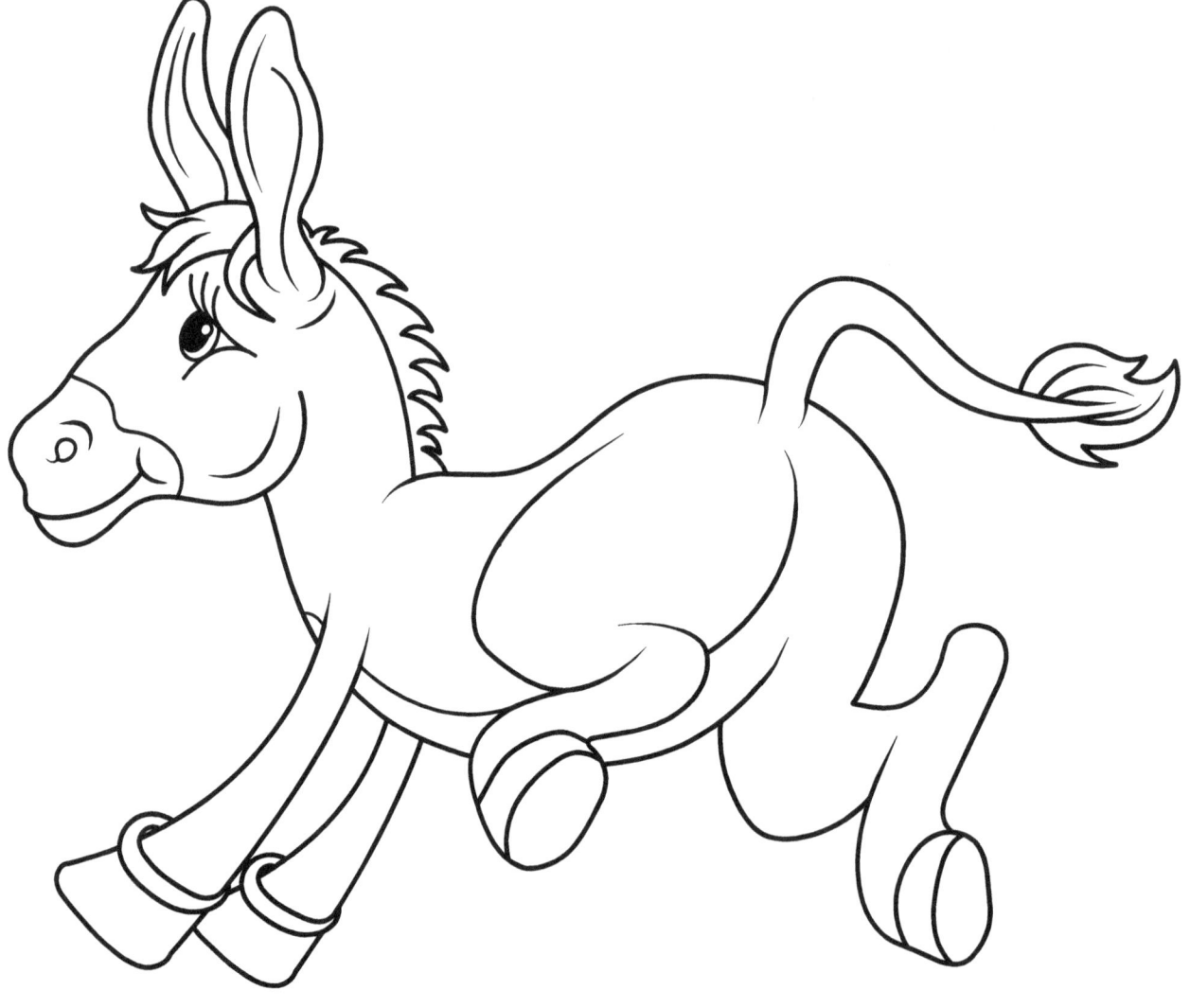

Cow

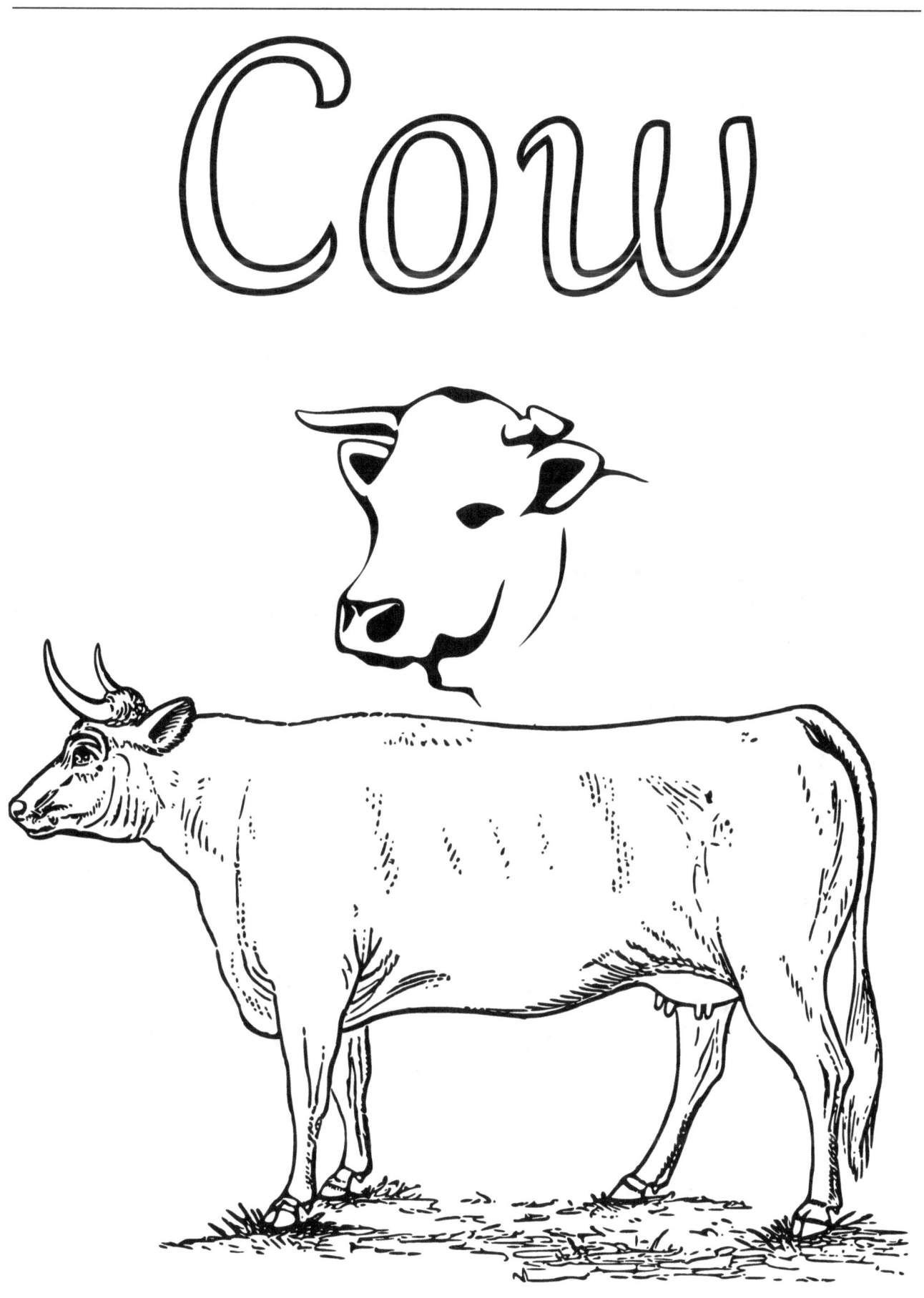

Sheep

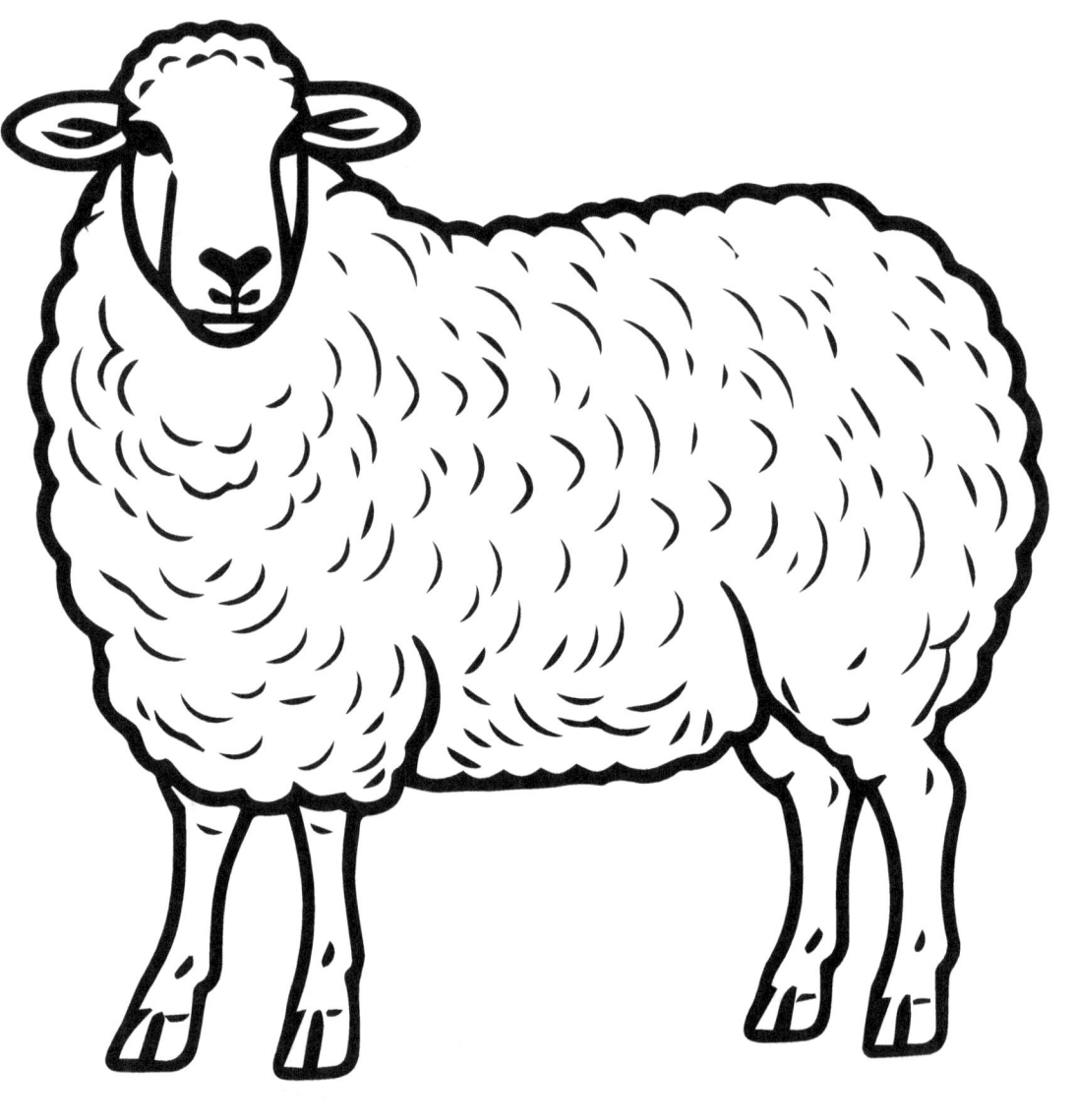

Goat

Dog

Cat

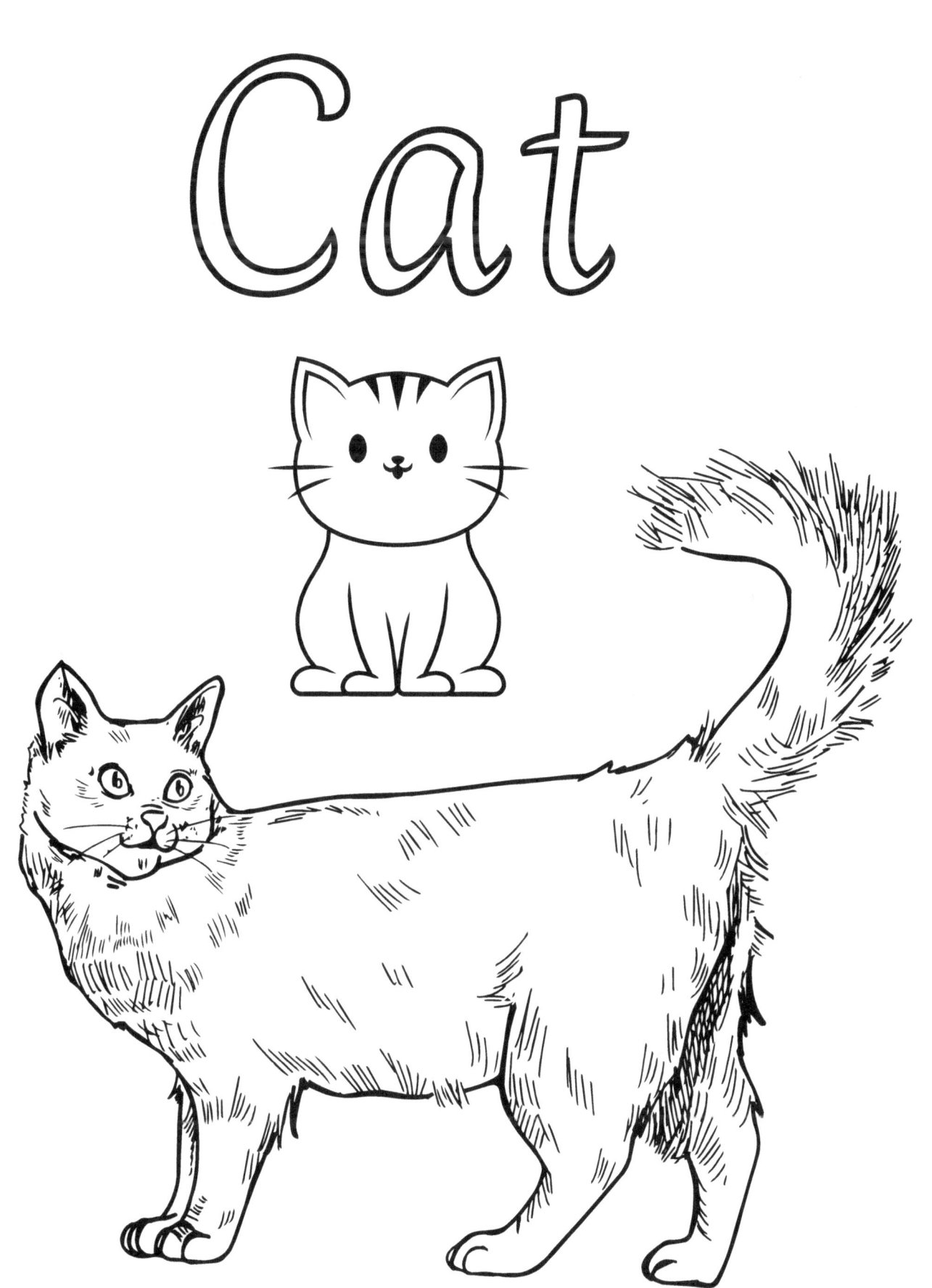

Rabbit

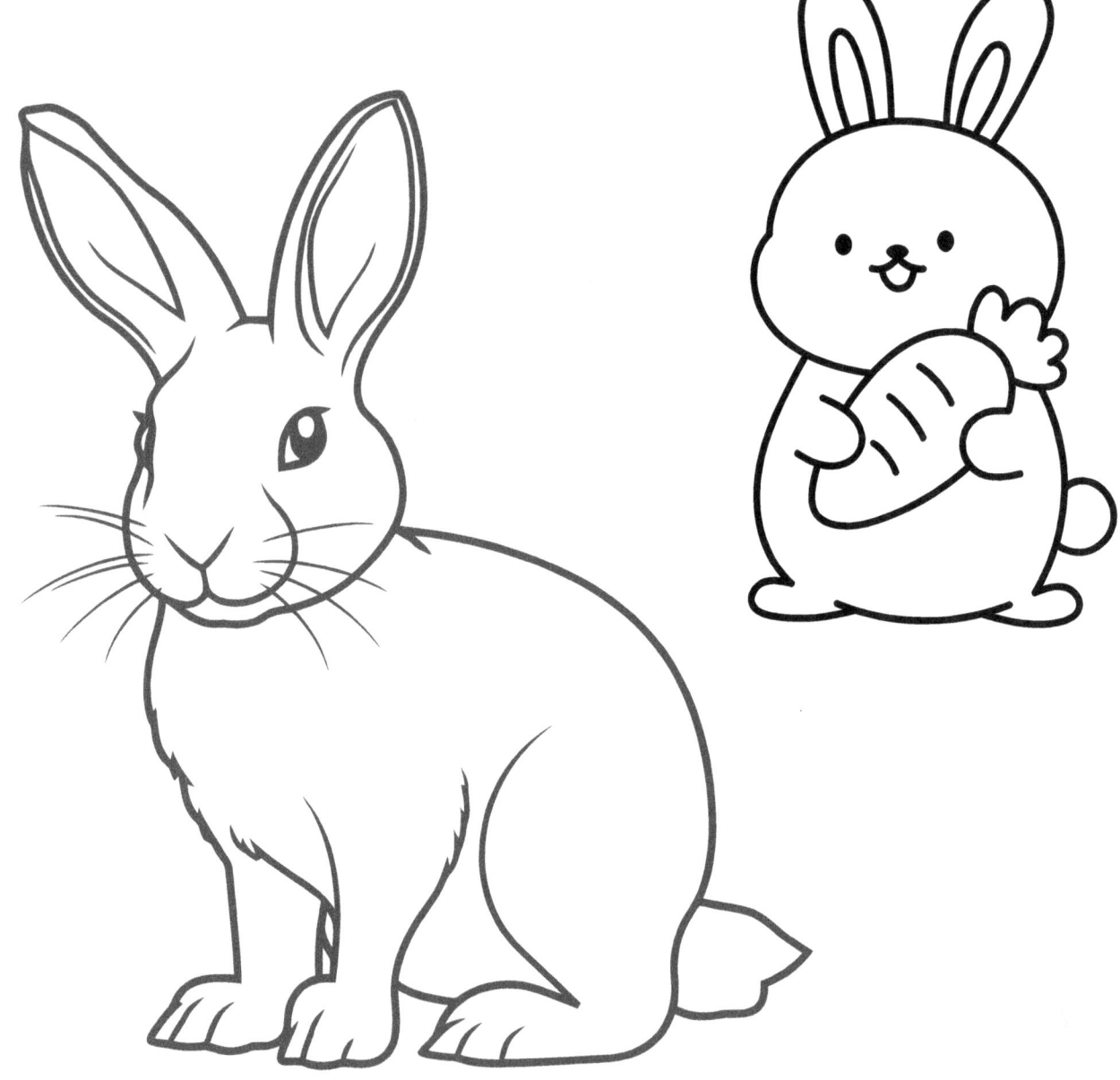

Rat

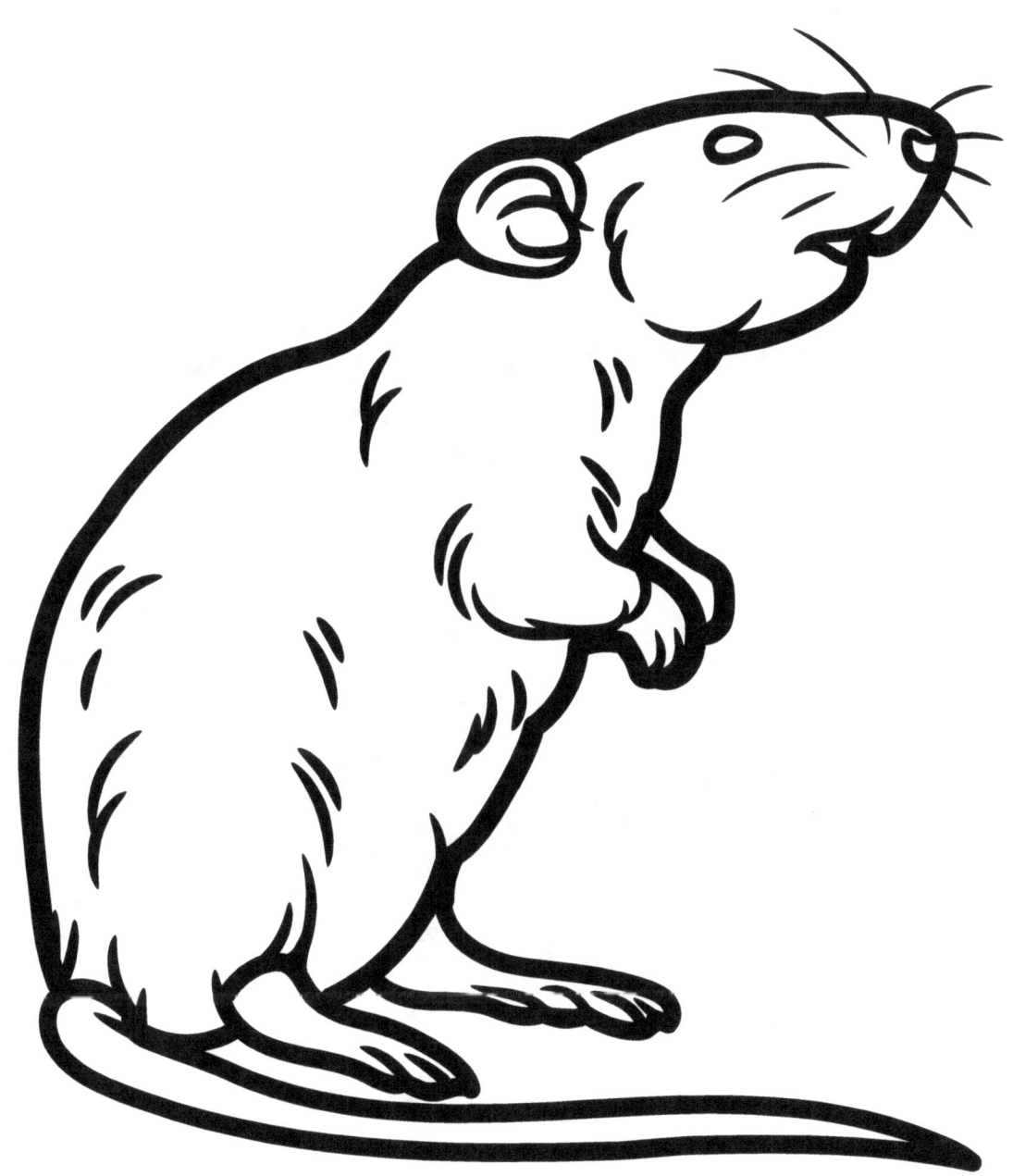

Mouse

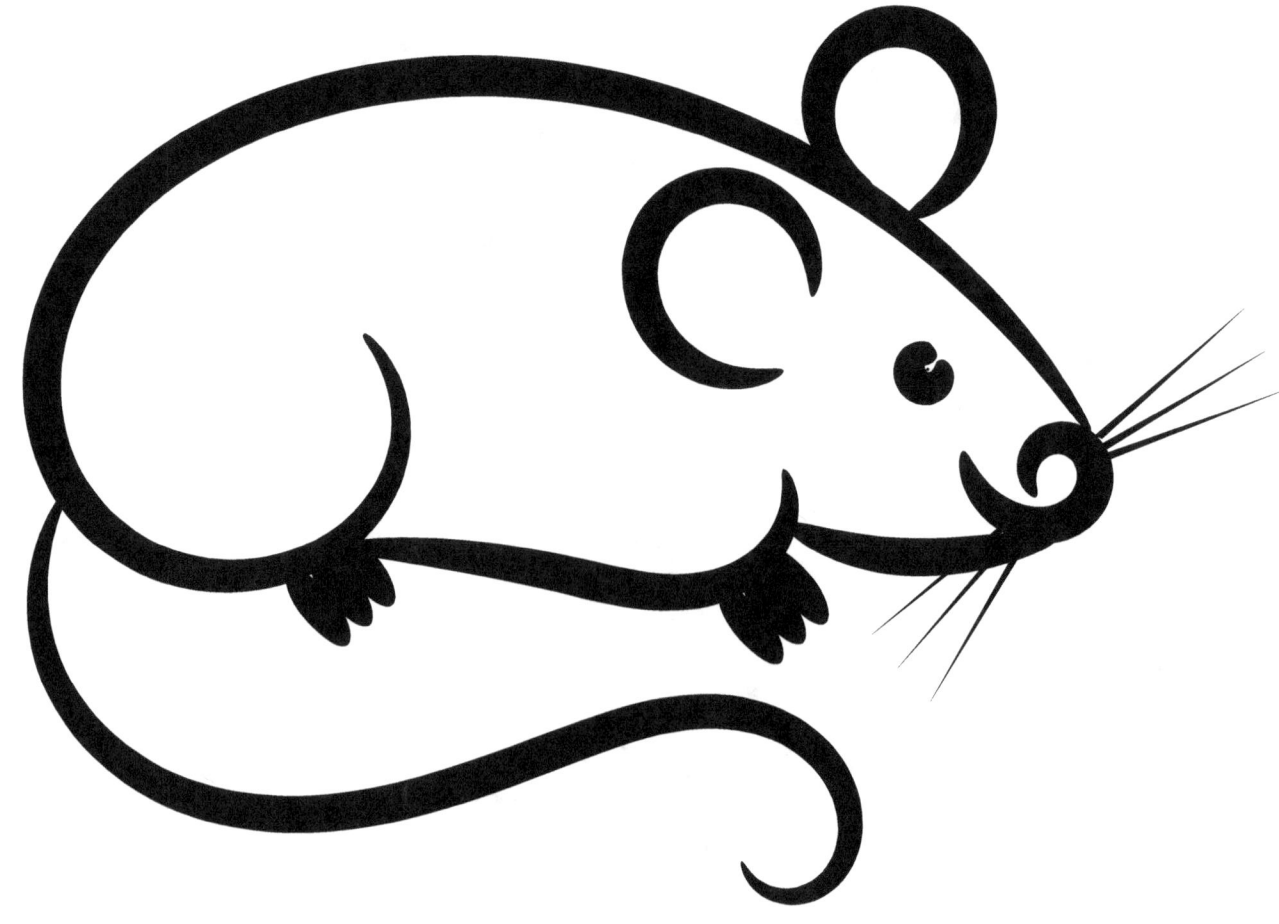

Eagle

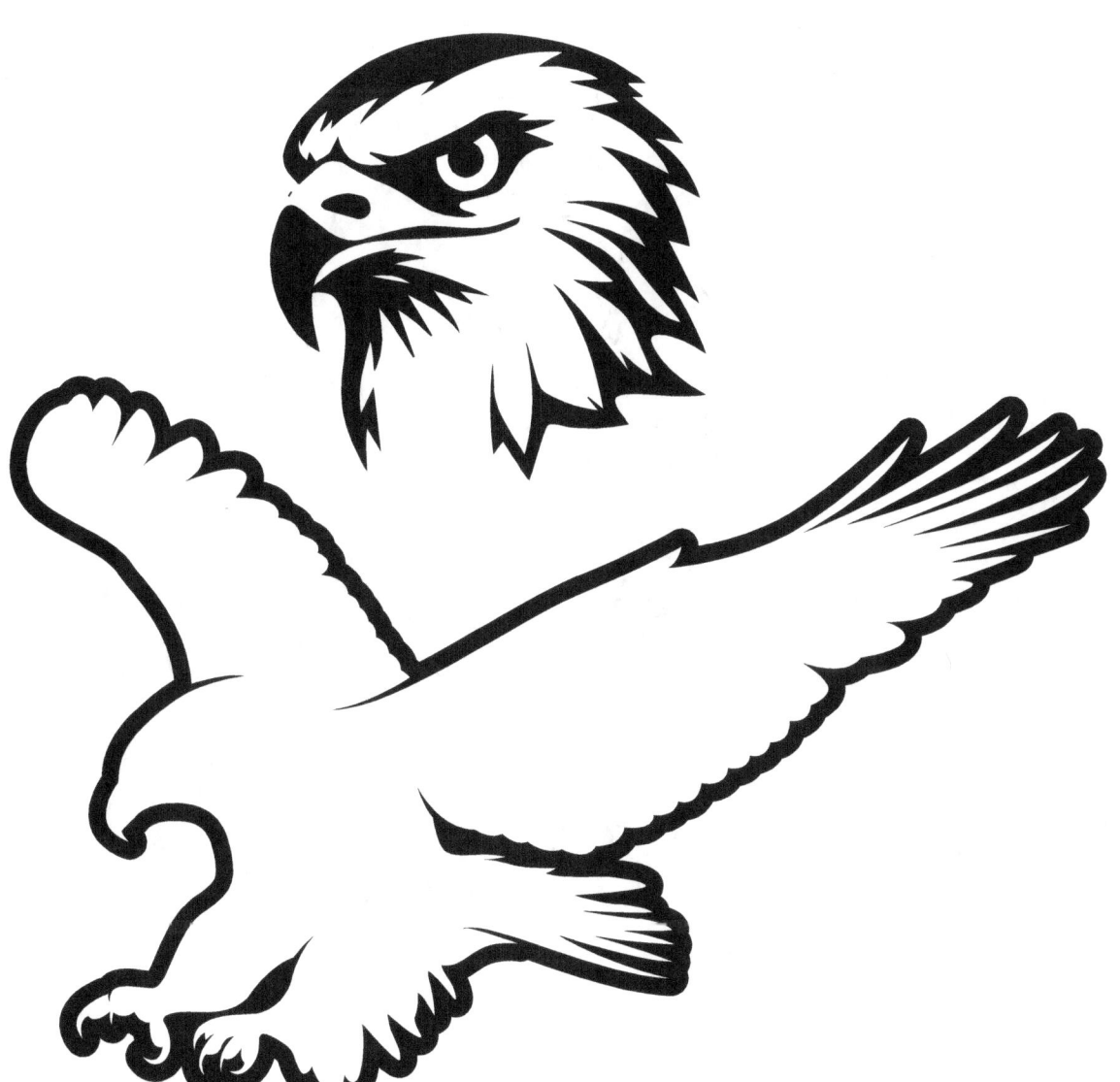

Parrot

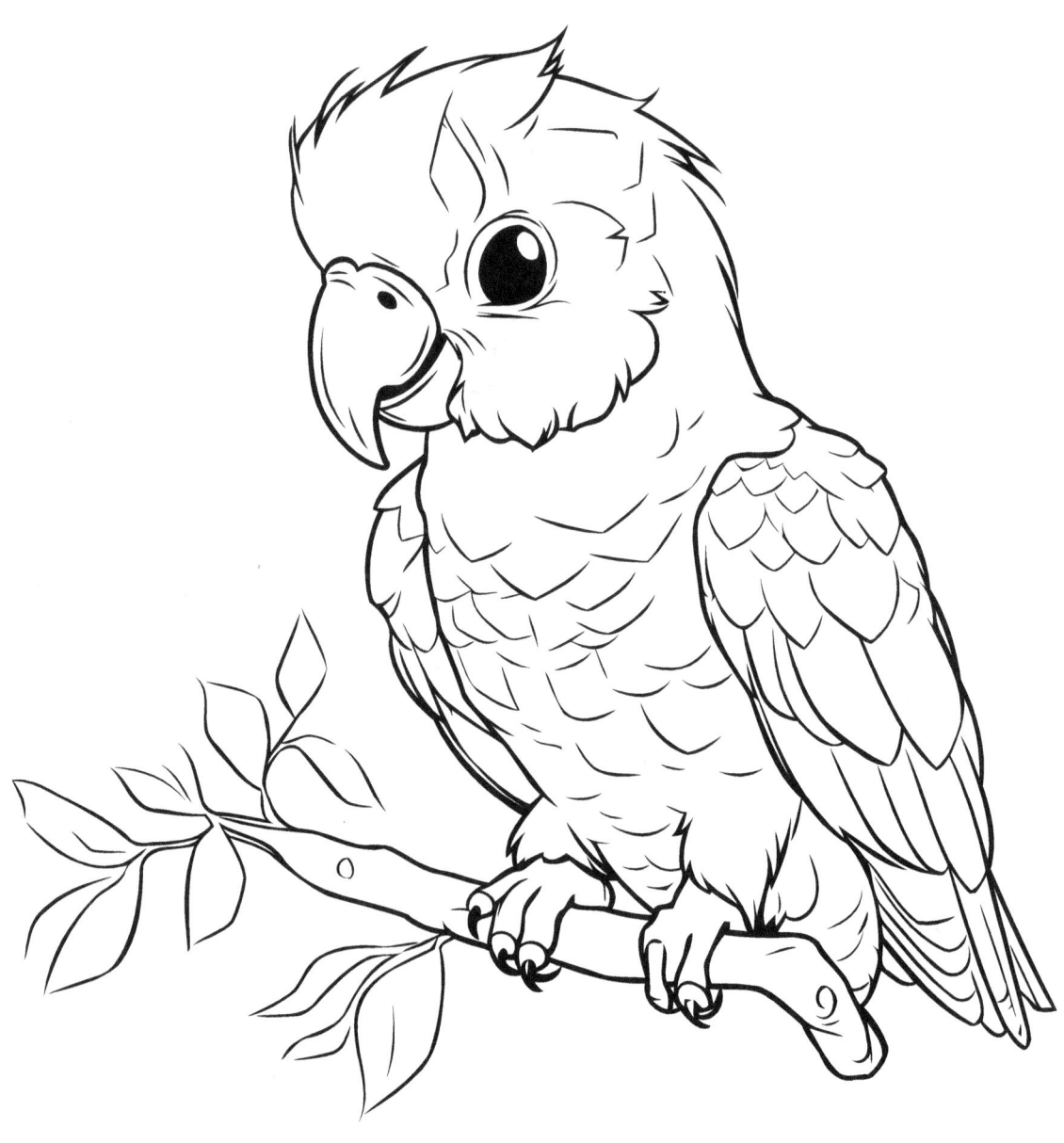

Dove

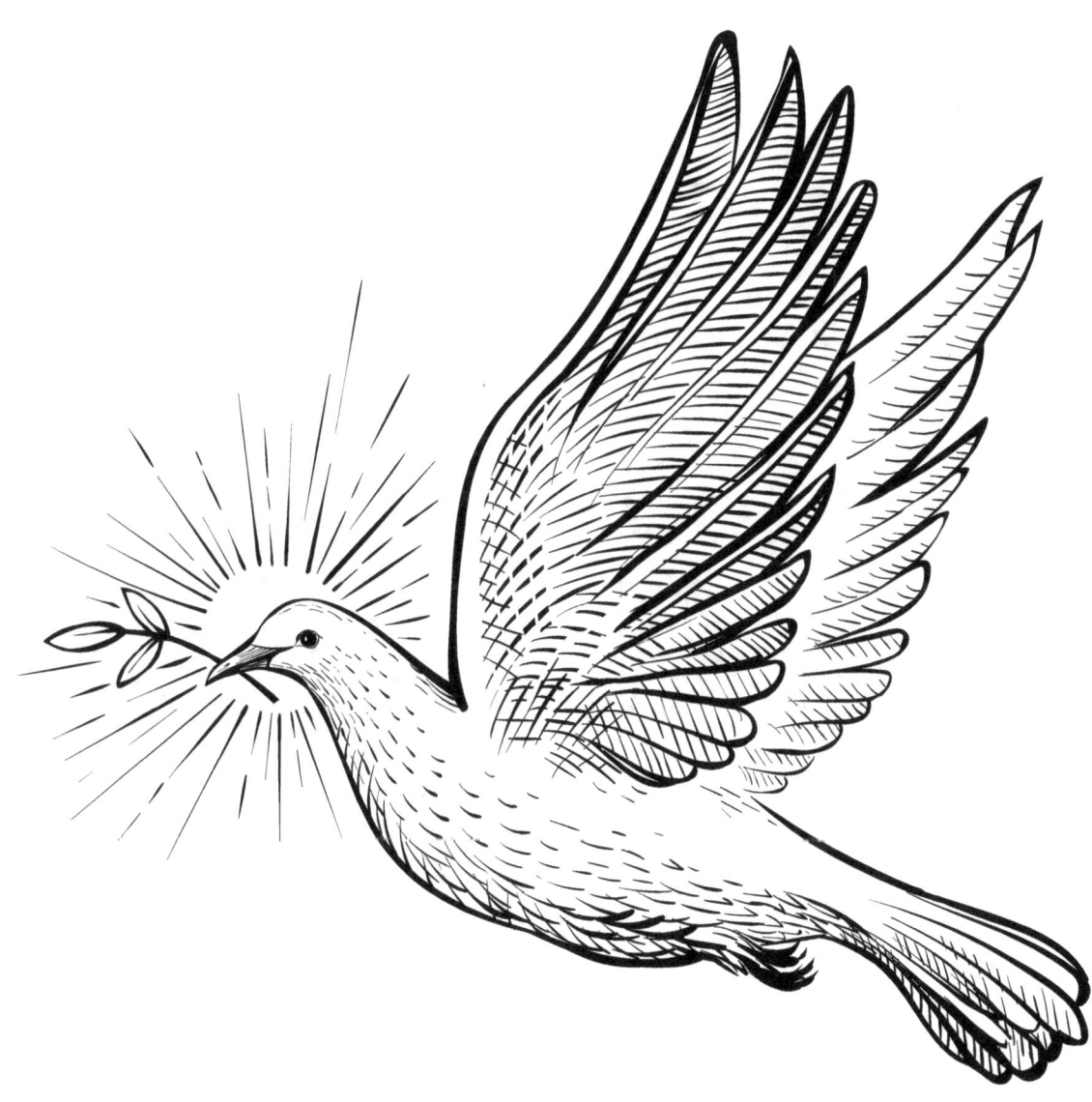

Peacock

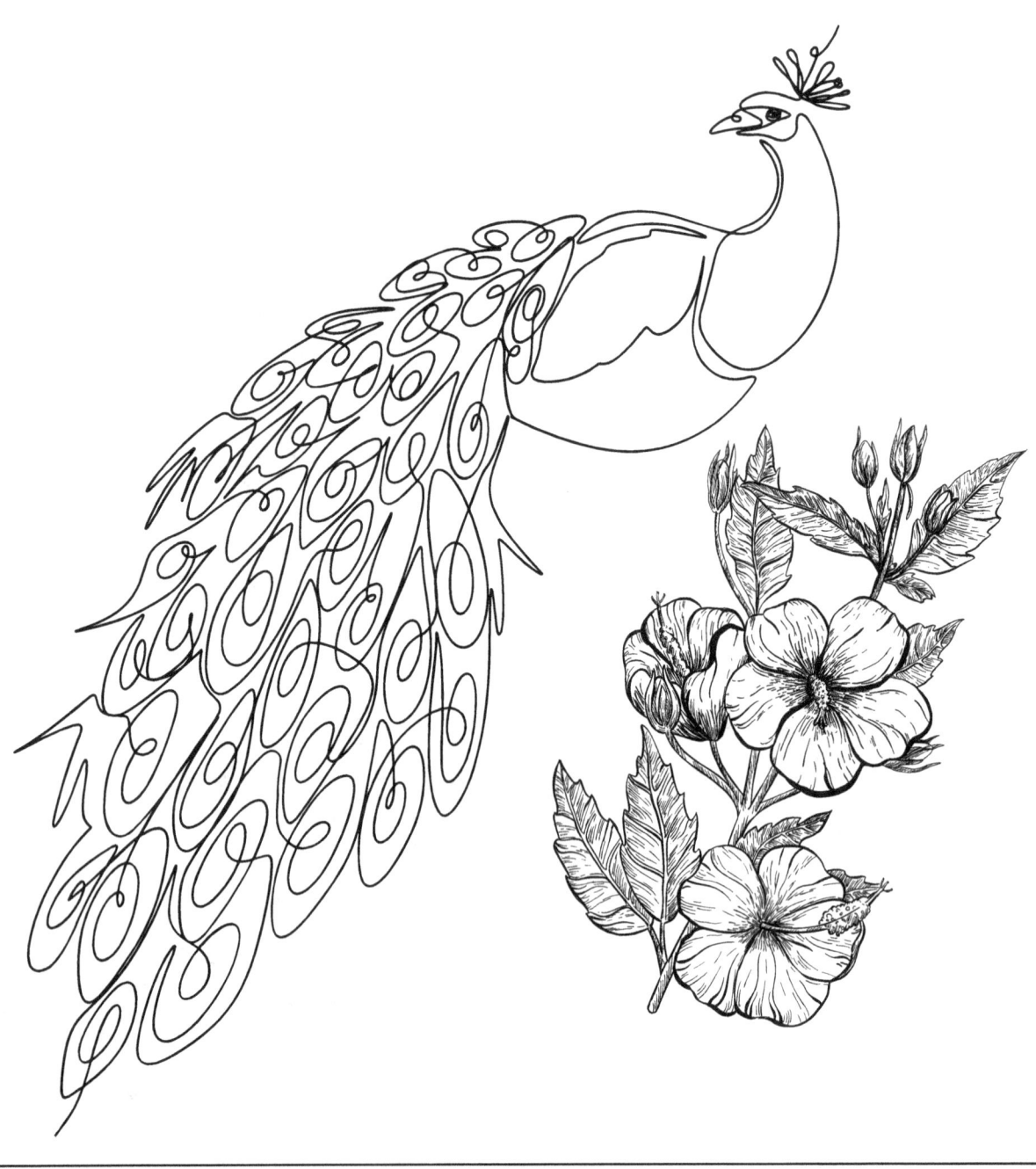

Penguin

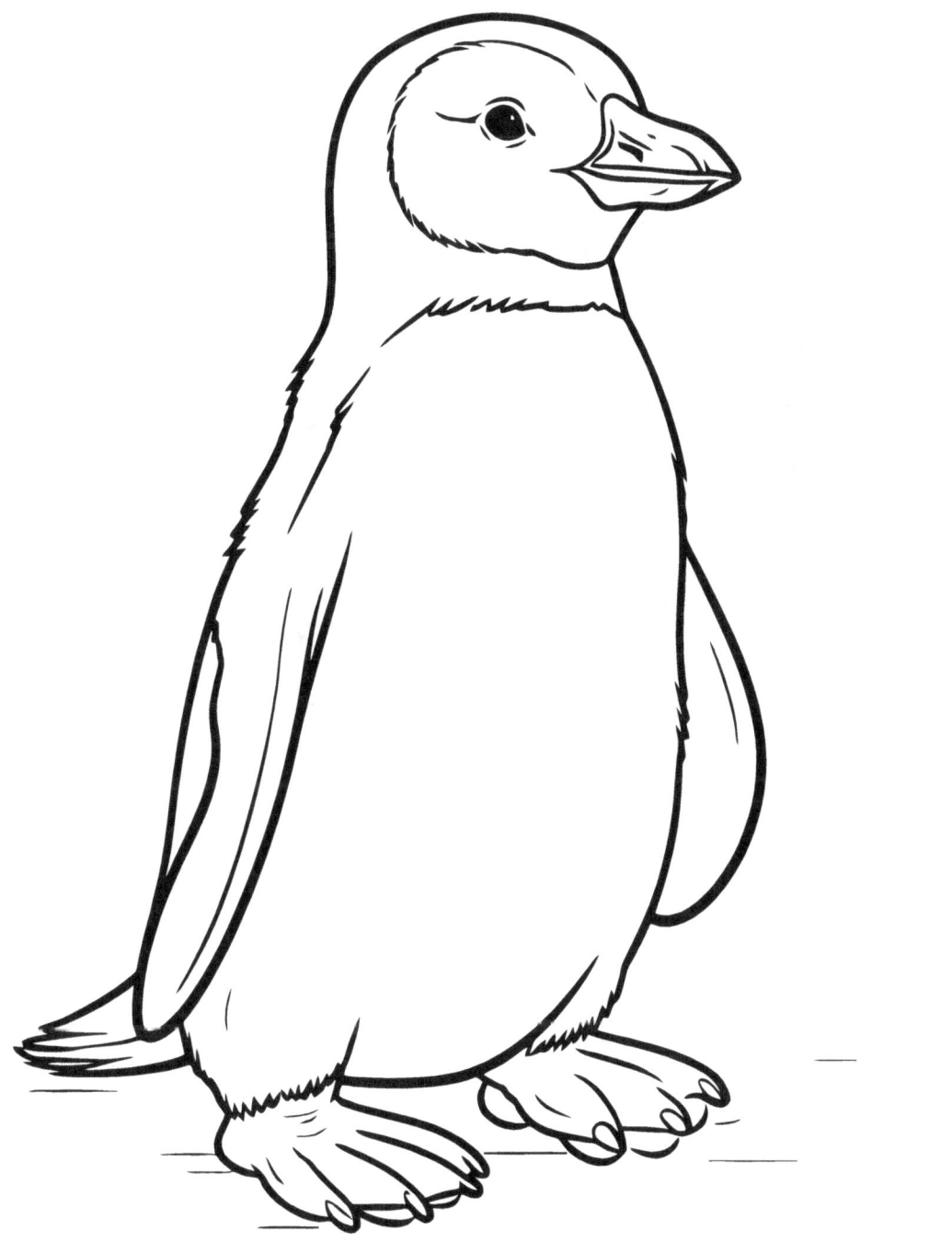

Ostrich

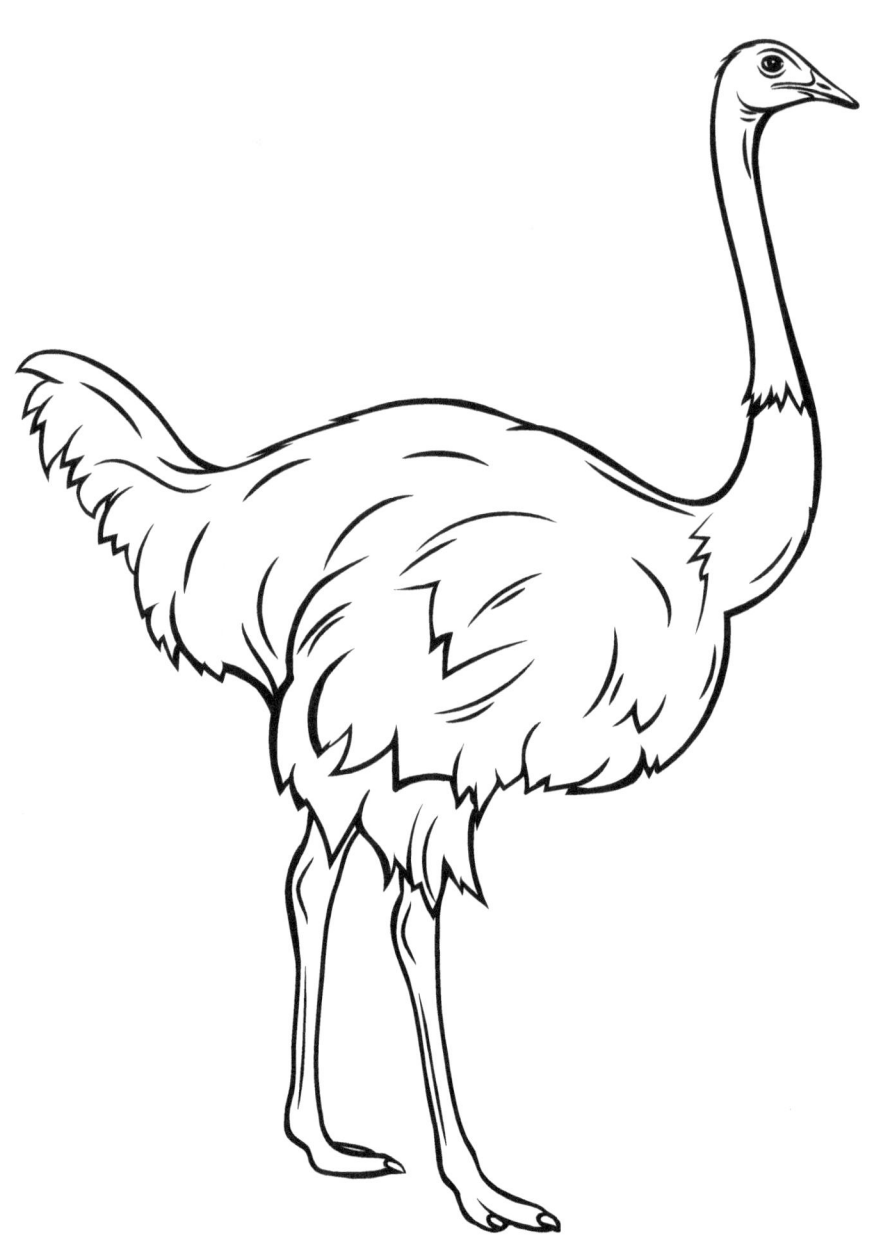

Kangaroo

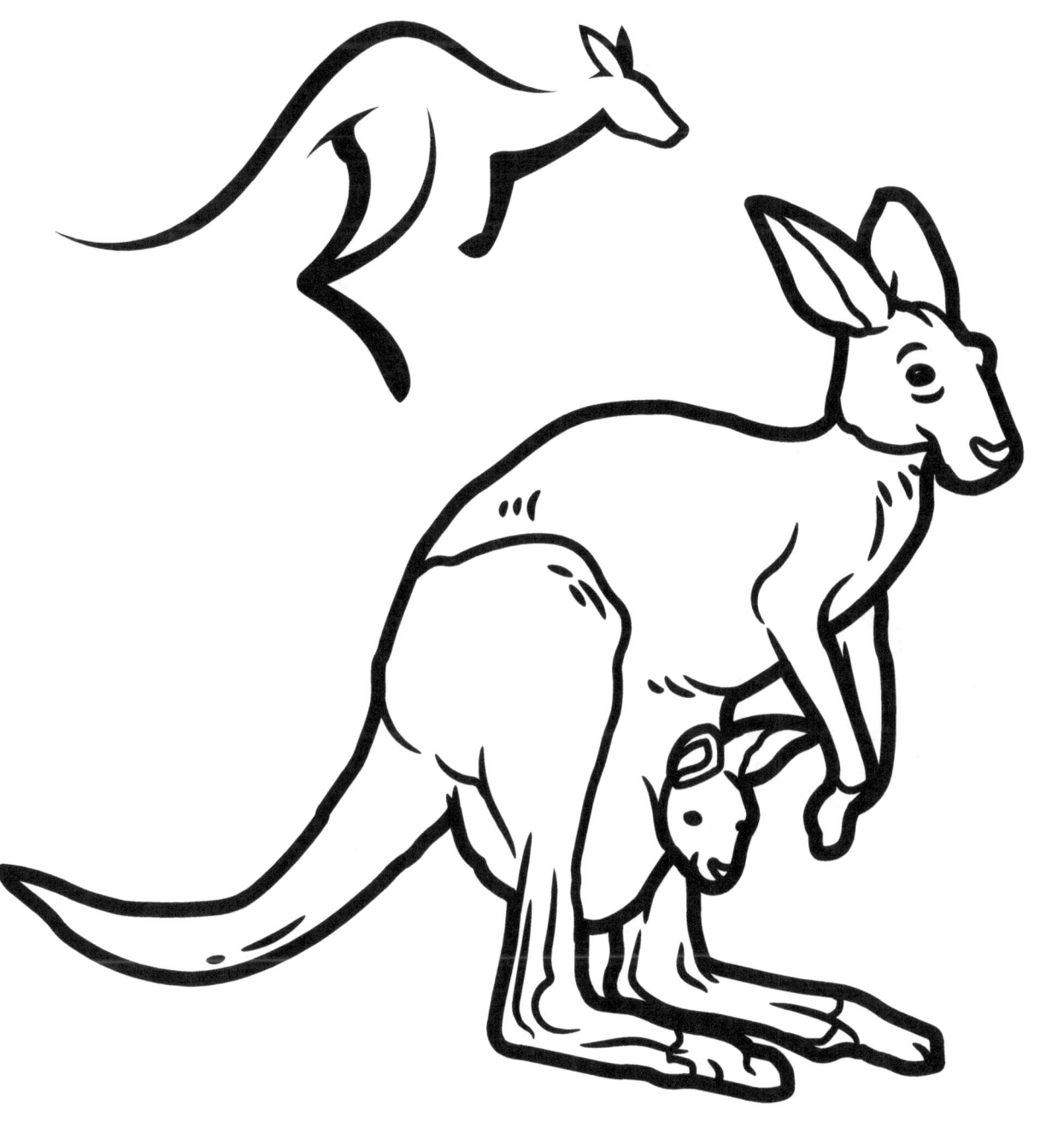

Koala

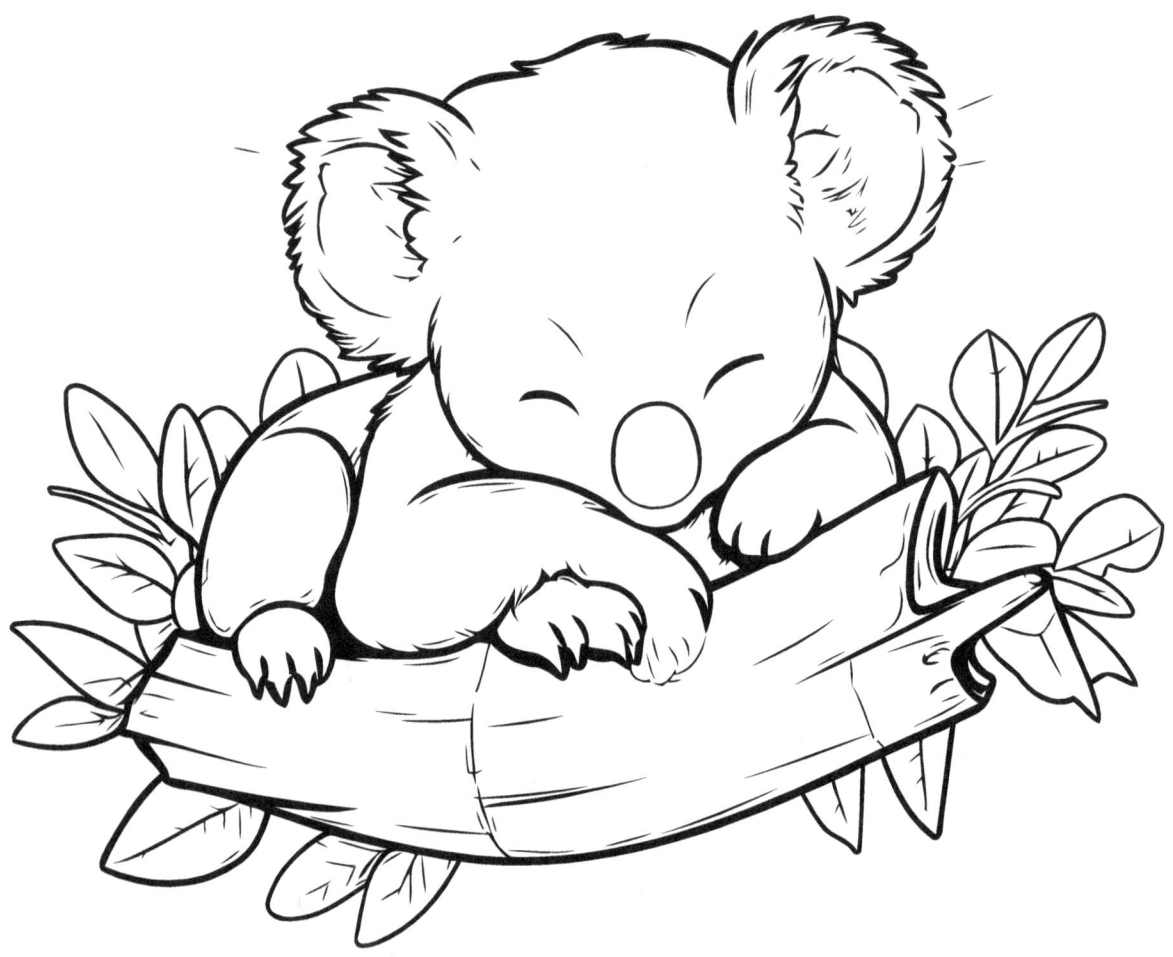

Monkey

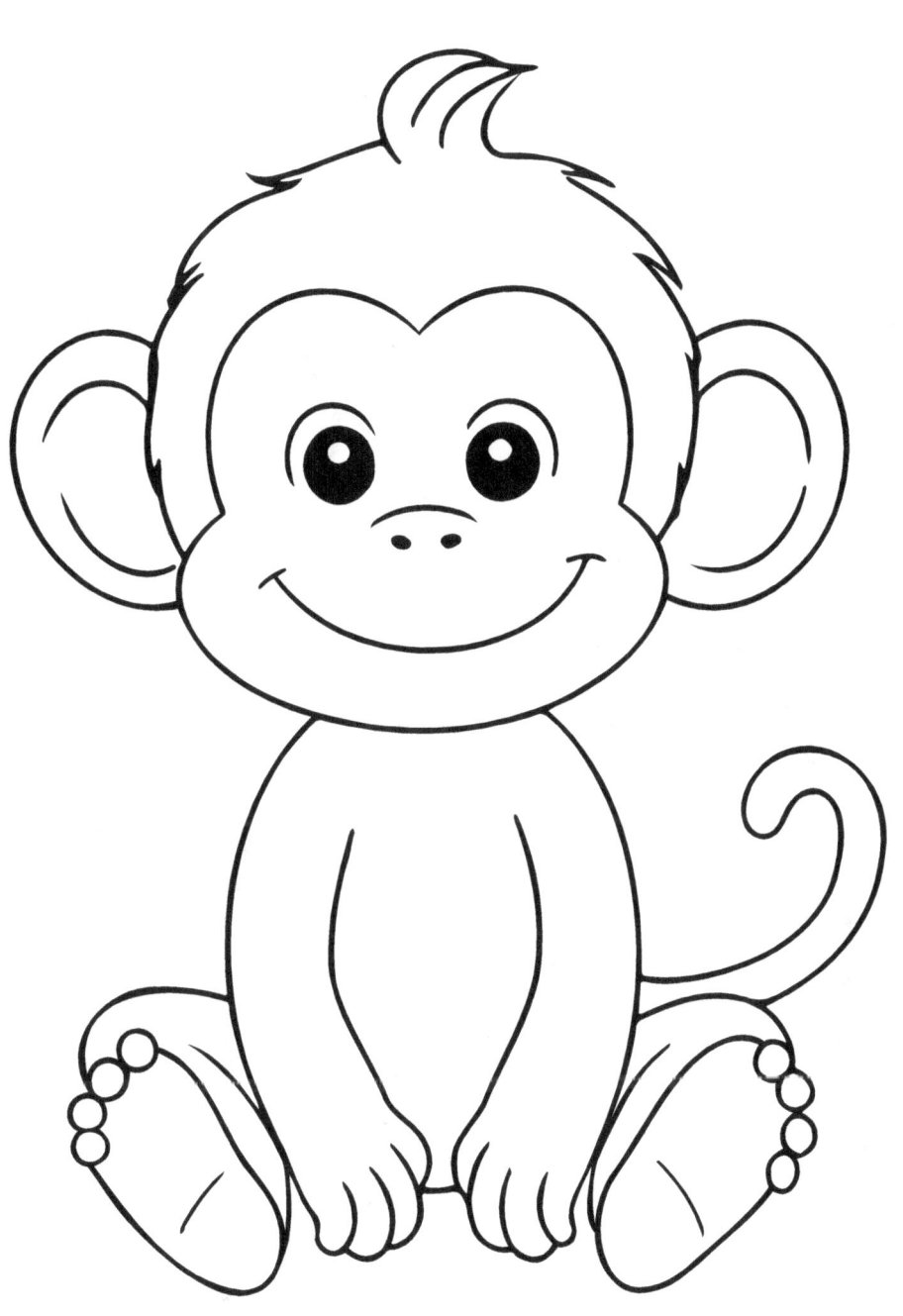

Gorilla

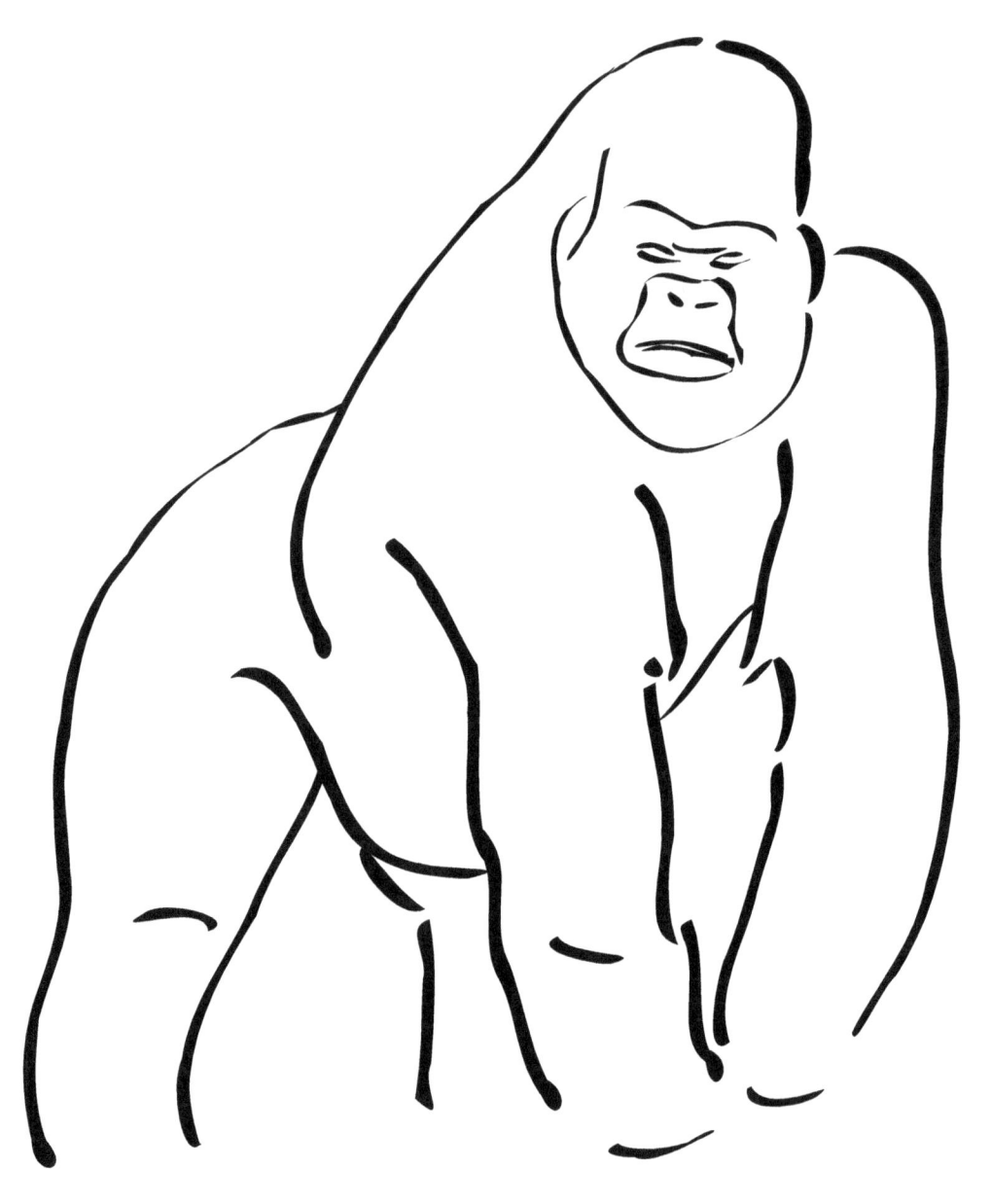

Crocodile

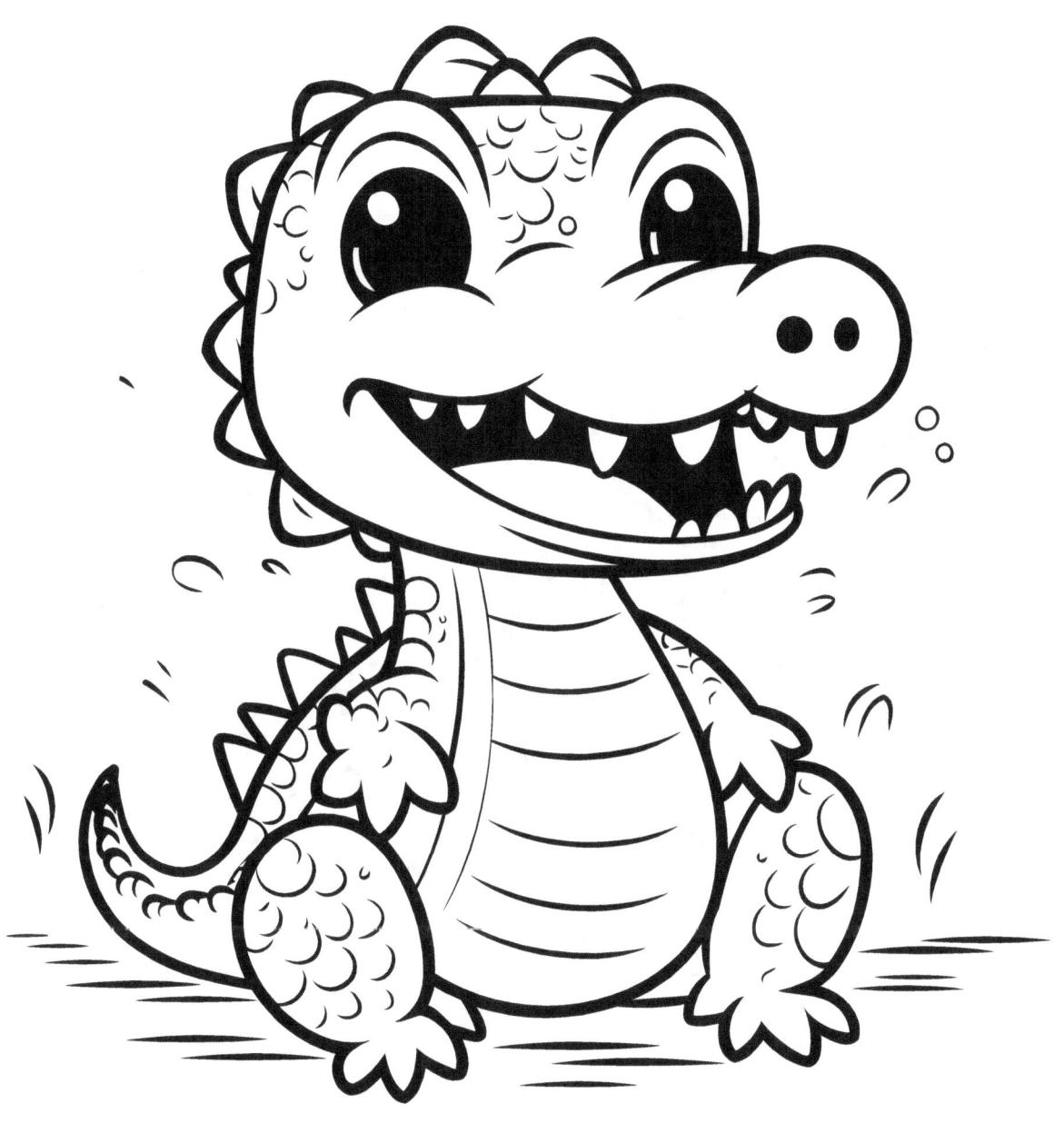

Turtle

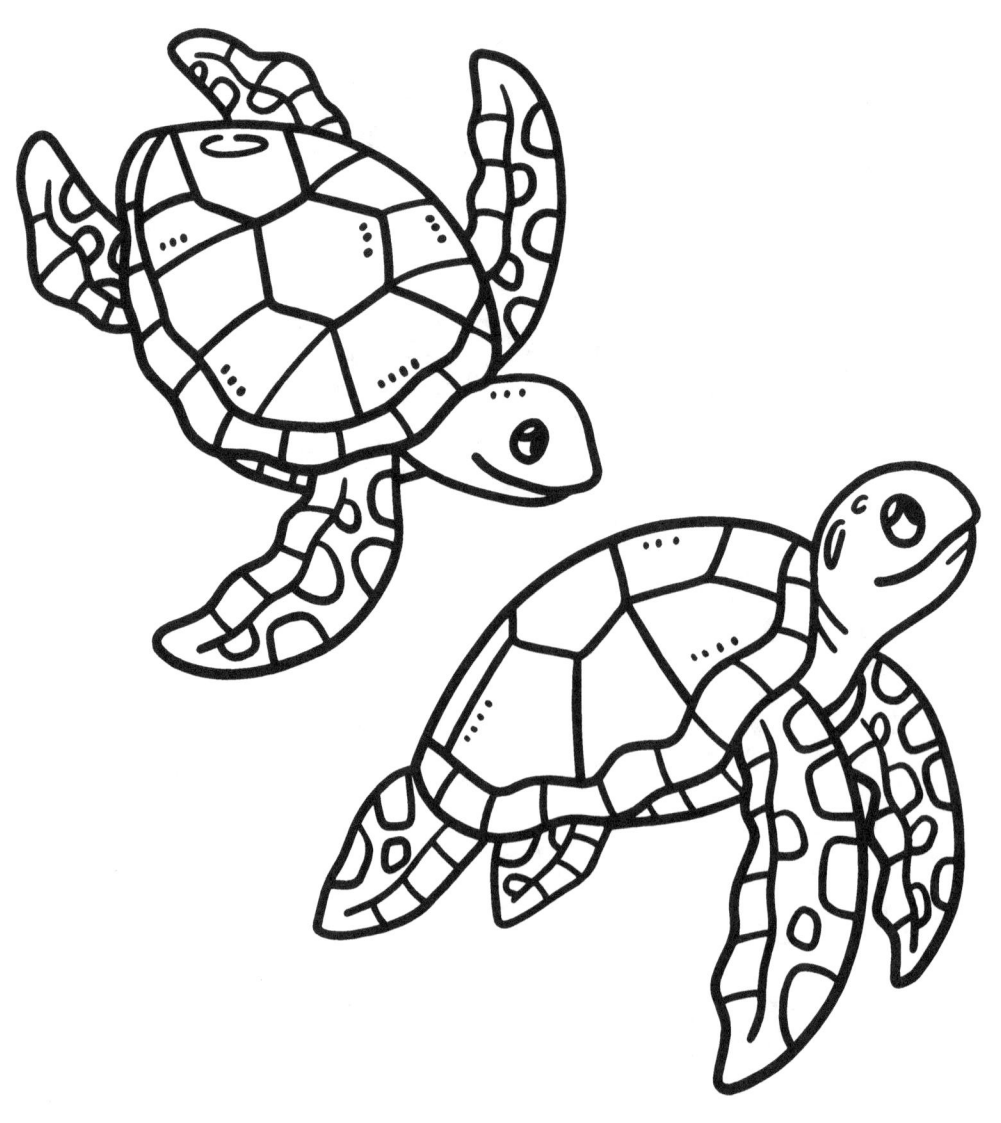

Snake

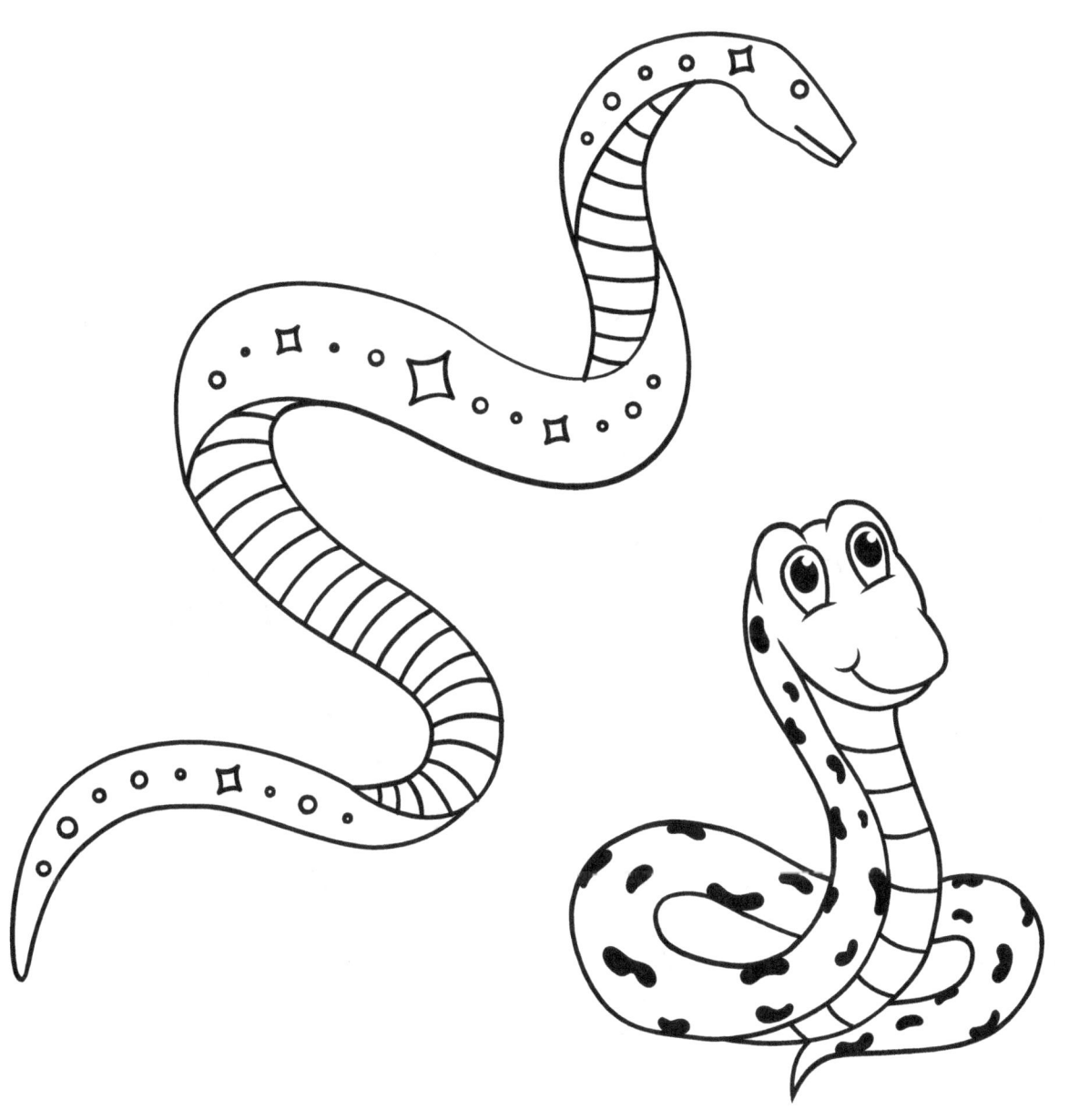

Lizard

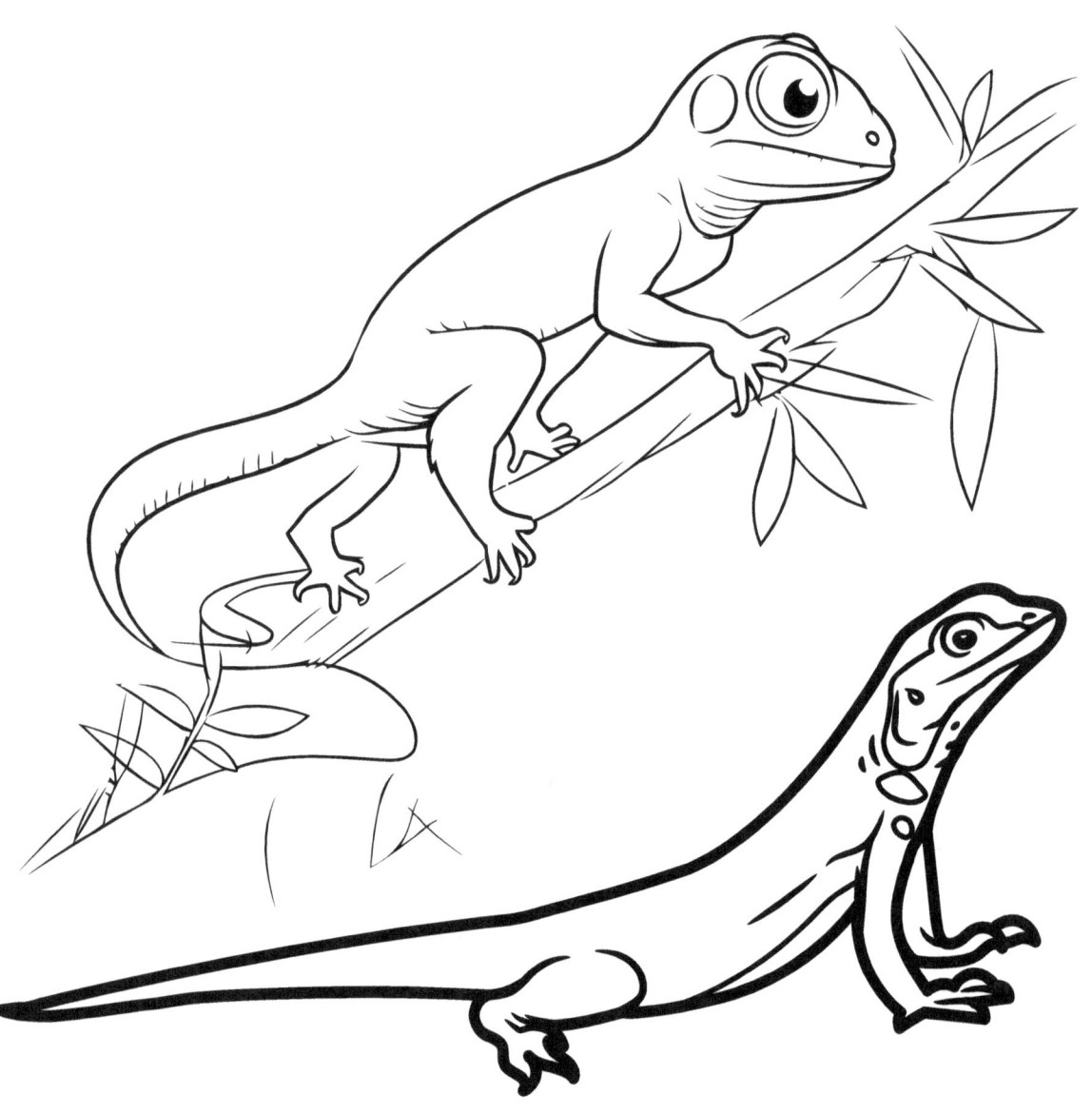

Frog

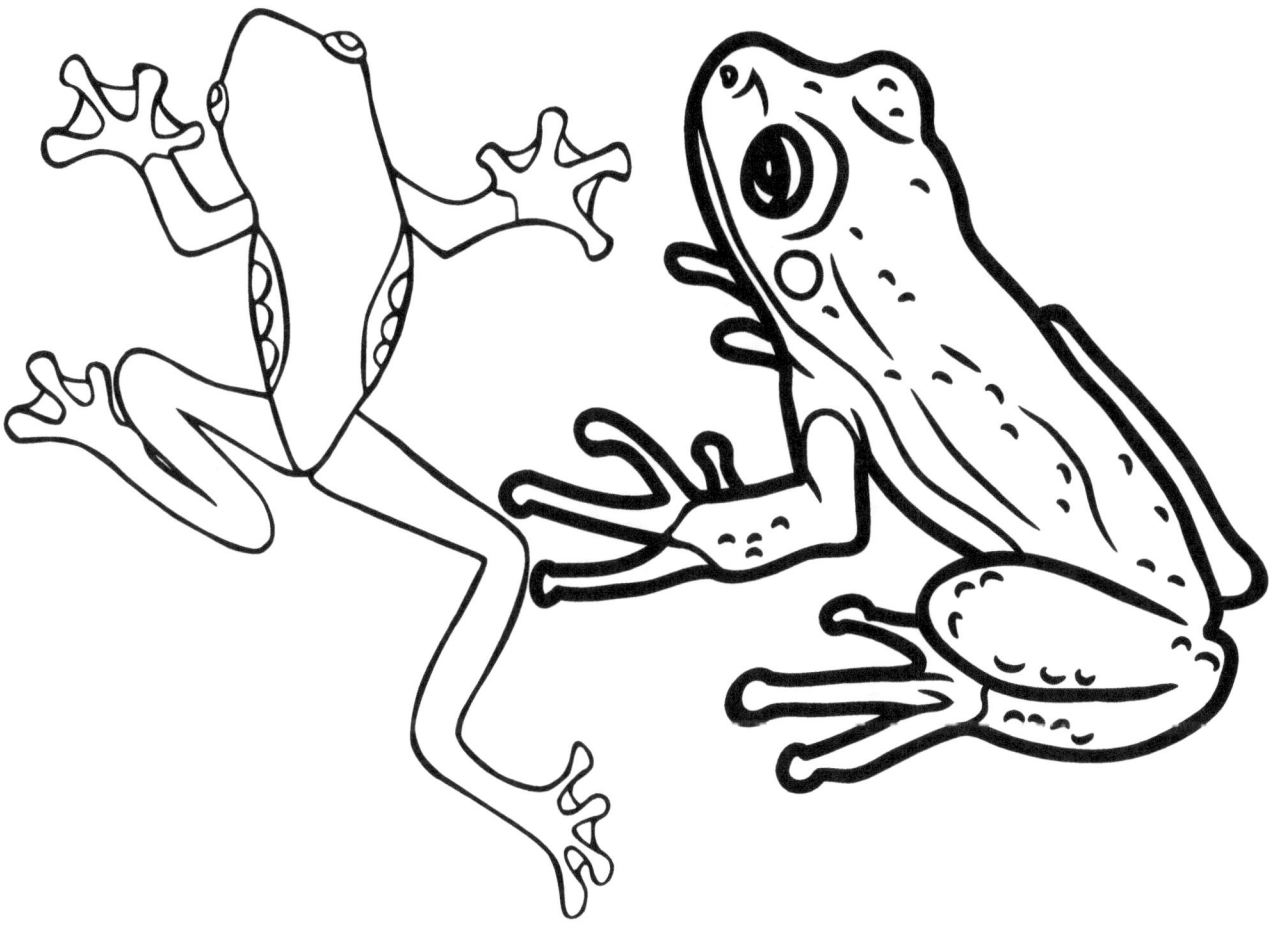